100 facts

Polar Lands

100 facts

Polar Lands

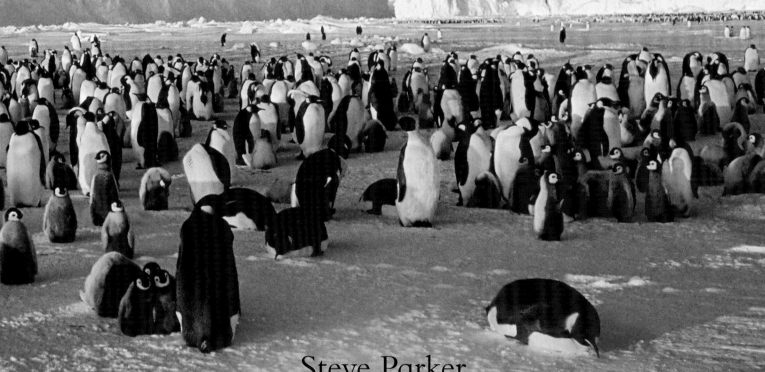

Steve Parker

Consultant: Camilla de la Bedoyere

Miles
Kelly

First published as hardback in 2008 by Miles Kelly Publishing Ltd
Harding's Barn, Bardfield End Green, Thaxted, Essex, CM6 3PX

Copyright © Miles Kelly Publishing Ltd 2008

This edition published 2014

4 6 8 10 9 7 5

Publishing Director: Belinda Gallagher
Creative Director: Jo Cowan
Senior Editor: Rosie Neave
Editorial Assistant: Chlöe Schroeter
Volume Designer: Sophie Pelham
Indexer: Gill Lee
Production Manager: Elizabeth Collins
Reprographics: Anthony Cambray, Jennifer Cozens, Ian Paulyn
Assets: Lorraine King

ISBN 978-1-84810-236-1

Printed in China

British Library Cataloguing-in-Publication Data
A catalogue record for this book is available from the British Library

ACKNOWLEDGEMENTS
The publishers would like to thank the following artists
who have contributed to this book:

Mike Foster, Adam Hook, Ian Jackson, Andrea Morandi

All other artworks from the Miles Kelly Artwork Bank

The publishers would like to thank the following sources for the use of their photographs:
Cover Michio Hoshino/Minden Pictures/FLPA; Page 6 Lehtikuva Oy/Rex Features; 10 Rob Howard/Corbis;
11 Matthias Breiter/Minden Pictures/FLPA; 12 Michio Hoshino/Minden Pictures/FLPA;
13 Patricio Robles Gil/Sierra Madre/Minden Pictures/FLPA; 14 Tom Bean/Corbis;
15 Sanford/Agliolo/Photolibrary; 18(t) Michio Hoshino/Minden Pictures/FLPA;
18(b) Jim Brandenburg/Minden Pictures/FLPA; 21 Michio Hoshino/Minden Pictures/FLPA;
22 Noel Hendrickson/Photolibrary; 24(t) Michael Quinton/Minden Pictures/FLPA; 24(b) Fritz Polking/FLPA;
26 Juniors Bildarchiv/Photolibrary; 28 Norbert WU/Minden Pictures/FLPA;
30 Wolfgang Kaehler/Corbis; 31(t) Fred Bruemmer/Still Pictures; 31(b) Paul A. Souders/Corbis;
32 Tim Davis/Photolibrary; 34 Bryan & Cherry Alexander Photography/Alamy;
35(t) Jack Jackson/Robert Harding World Imagery/Corbis; 35(b) Patrick Robert/Corbis; 37(t) Galen Rowell/Corbis;
37(b) Bryan & Cherry Alexander/NHPA; 38 Bryan & Cherry Alexander/NHPA;
39 Bryan & Cherry Alexander Photography/Alamy; 40 Stapleton Collection/Corbis;
41 Jason Roberts/Push Pictures/Handout/epa/Corbis; 42 ©TopFoto TopFoto.co.uk;
43 Van Hasselt John/Corbis Sygma; 44 Paul Souders/Corbis; 45(t) Toby Zerna/Newspix/Rex Features;
45(b) Bruno P. Zehnder/Still Pictures; 46 Colin Monteath/Minden Pictures/FLPA

All other photographs are from:
Corel, digitalSTOCK, digitalvision, iStockphoto.com, John Foxx, PhotoAlto,
PhotoDisc, PhotoEssentials, PhotoPro, Stockbyte

Made with paper from a sustainable forest

www.mileskelly.net   info@mileskelly.net

Contents

It's cold at the Poles!

1 **The polar regions are found at the top and bottom of the Earth and they are the coldest, windiest places in the world.** Here, the land and sea stay frozen for most of the year, and snow and ice stretch as far as the eye can see. Only a few creatures are tough enough to survive these frozen conditions.

▼ Ice-breakers like the *Apu* have enough power to smash through metre-thick ice in polar seas. They clear the way for following ships, which must keep up because the ice re-freezes in a few hours.

The ends of the Earth

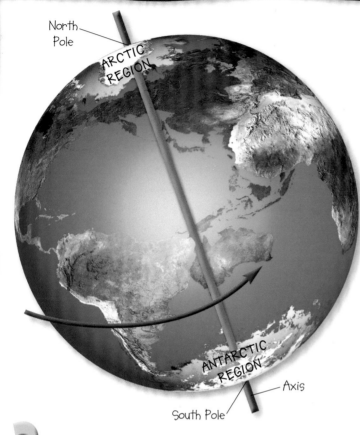

North Pole

ARCTIC REGION

ANTARCTIC REGION

Axis

South Pole

3 **The Earth really has four poles!** There are the Geographic North and South Poles, which are defined by the position of the Earth's axis, but there are also the Magnetic North and South Poles. The Magnetic Poles are some distance from the Geographic Poles.

◀ The Earth spins around an imaginary line called the axis, which passes through the Geographic North and South Poles.

4 **The Earth is like a giant magnet.** Deep inside the Earth are layers of hot, liquid metals, especially iron. As the Earth turns, the iron moves, creating a magnetic force. The Magnetic Poles are the two places where this force is strongest.

Antarctic Peninsula

2 **The North and South Poles are at the top and bottom of the Earth.** Every 24 hours, Earth turns once around its axis. The axis is an invisible line that runs through the middle (core) of the Earth, from Pole to Pole.

Lines of magnetic force

◀ These lines show the pulling power of the Earth's magnetic core.

5 **Because of the moving liquid metals inside the Earth, the magnetic poles wander, and may move a few metres every year.** Throughout history, the poles have flipped. This is known as magnetic reversal – the Magnetic North Pole becomes the Magnetic South Pole, and the Magnetic South Pole becomes the Magnetic North Pole. The last flip was about 780,000 years ago.

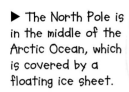

▶ The North Pole is in the middle of the Arctic Ocean, which is covered by a floating ice sheet.

ARCTIC OCEAN
(ice sheet)

Geographic North Pole
✷

GREENLAND

6 **The northern polar region is called the Arctic.** The word *Arctic* comes from the ancient Greek word *arktos*, meaning 'bear'. This refers to the star pattern (constellation) called the Little Bear, or *Ursa Minor*. It contains a star near the North Pole, known as the Pole Star.

Geographic South Pole
✷

ANTARCTICA

◀ ▼ The South Pole is towards one side of the vast, ice-covered land mass of Antarctica. In early April penguins gather at traditonal breeding sites on the sea ice.

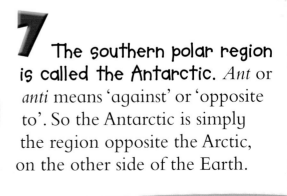

I DON'T BELIEVE IT!

Antarctica is the coldest place on Earth. At Vostok Base, the coldest-ever temperature was –89°C in 1983. That's more than four times colder than inside a freezer!

SOUTHERN OCEAN

7 The southern polar region is called the Antarctic. *Ant* or *anti* means 'against' or 'opposite to'. So the Antarctic is simply the region opposite the Arctic, on the other side of the Earth.

Extreme seasons

8 **The Earth's axis is not completely vertical.** It is tilted at angle of around 23°. The movement of the Earth around the Sun, combined with this angle, gives our world its seasons.

▲ At the North Pole, the Sun never disappears below the horizon at Midsummer's Day.

9 **The Earth moves around (orbits) the Sun.** Over the course of a year, first one and then the other Pole leans towards the Sun, giving us seasons.

▼ Midnight Sun (the presence of the Sun throughout the night), means that people can travel at any time, day or night.

10 **In most polar lands, summer is long and light, and on some days the Sun never sets.** Winter is long and dark, and on some days the Sun never rises. The further north or south you are in the world, the more extreme the seasons will be.

11 When the North Pole is facing away from the Sun, the area around it is in perpetual darkness. The Sun does not rise for at least one night in midwinter. This area is known as the Arctic Circle. The Antarctic Circle is a similar area around the South Pole. When it is midwinter in the Arctic it is midsummer in Antarctica, so at the Antarctic Circle, the Sun does not set for at least one day.

12 Sometimes at night, the polar skies are lit by shimmering, waving curtains of multi-coloured lights. These are called the *Aurora Borealis* or Northern Lights in the Arctic. Around Antarctica they are called the *Aurora Australis* or Southern Lights.

▼ Campers in the forests of the far north see the Northern Lights as a wavy glow. Tonight it is yellow-green. Tomorrow it may be blue or red!

NO SUNSET

You will need:
an apple   a desk lamp

Imagine your apple is the Earth, and the lamp is the Sun. The stem of the apple represents the North Pole. Hold the apple in front of the lamp and angle the stem towards the light. Spin the apple around its core. Despite the spinning, the area around the North Pole has light all the time, while the other side stays in darkness. This illustrates midsummer at the Arctic Circle.

13 The lights are made by tiny particles given off by the Sun, known as the solar wind. These get trapped by the Earth's magnetism and start to glow. This happens very high in the sky, above 100 kilometres, which is three times higher than a passenger jet plane can travel.

Land around a frozen sea

14 The Arctic is a mostly frozen area of the Arctic Ocean that is surrounded by land. The Arctic Ocean is the smallest, shallowest ocean, with an area of about 14 million square kilometres, and an average depth of 1000 metres. During winter, the ice over the ocean becomes up to 3 metres thick. In summer it shrinks, but it never disappears.

▶ In spring, enormous herds of caribou (reindeer) migrate north to feed on the plants of the tundra.

15 The floating ice layer over the Arctic Ocean cracks and melts around the edges to form dangerous pack ice (icebergs) and icefields. Around the shores of the Arctic Ocean, massive lumps of ice break from ice sheets and form glaciers (frozen rivers), which float out into the ocean as icebergs.

16 Around the Arctic Ocean it is too cold and windy for any trees to grow. The main plants are tussock grass, small bushes, low-growing mosses and lichens. These treeless zones are known as tundra. The Arctic hares that live here have very short ears, to stop them losing body heat.

17

Around the tundra, millions of conifers form huge areas known as boreal forests, or taiga. These are some of Earth's last unexplored wildernesses. Conifer trees' needle-like leaves and downward-sloping branches mean that snow slides off easily. If too much snow gathered, the branches would become heavy and break.

18

The deer known as caribou in North America are called reindeer in northern Europe and Asia. They wander through the forests in winter, then trek out to tundra areas for the summer, in long journeys known as migrations. Packs of wolves follow them and pick off the old, young, sick and dying.

19

In some Arctic regions, the soil just below the surface never thaws, even in summer. These areas are called permafrost. The layer of ice does not let surface water drain through down into the soil below. So permafrost areas are usually boggy and swampy.

FLOATING ICEBERG

Icebergs are much bigger than they look. Make a big lump of ice by putting a plastic bowl of water into a freezer. Float this lump in a sink filled with water. How much is above the surface? In an iceberg it is usually about one-eighth of the total volume above, leaving seven-eighths below.

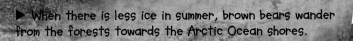

▶ When there is less ice in summer, brown bears wander from the forests towards the Arctic Ocean shores.

Sea around a frozen land

20 **Antarctica is different to the Arctic in many ways.** The Arctic is a sea surrounded by land, while the Antarctic is land surrounded by sea. Antarctica is a huge landmass about 14 million square kilometres in area, mostly covered by ice. It has mountains, valleys, and old volcanoes, but nearly all of these are hidden under the ice.

Corrie (bowl)

Glacier

Crevasses (cracks)

Melting nose or snout

Squeezed snow and ice

▶ Snow and ice slide slowly from the polar ice caps as long glaciers, down to the sea.

21 **Around Antarctica is the Southern Ocean, also called the Antarctic or Southern Polar Ocean.** It is larger and deeper than the Arctic Ocean, with an area of around 20 million square kilometres and an average depth of 4500 metres. It merges into southern parts of the Atlantic, Indian and Pacific Oceans.

◀ Massive chunks split off the ice cap into the sea, and float away as they melt.

22 During the long, dark winter, the Antarctic ice sheet spreads into the surrounding ocean. It forms layers known as ice shelves, which float on the surface. As summer arrives, the shelves shrink back again.

23 Huge ice blocks break off the ice shelves to form massive icebergs. This ice was originally snow, so it is made of fresh water. It differs from the sea ice that forms in the middle of the Arctic Ocean.

24 Each summer, a small area of Antarctica becomes ice-free. This is mainly along the Antarctic Peninsula towards South America. The land is mostly rock and thin soil, where only a few small plants and animals can survive.

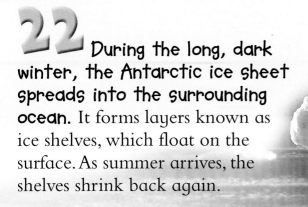

I DON'T BELIEVE IT!

Antarctica's ice cap is an average of 1600 metres deep. In places the ice goes down 3350 metres before reaching the rocky surface of the continent. Here there are streams, rivers and lakes, all far below the ice surface.

▶ Most of an iceberg is hidden below the sea's surface, and sometimes scrapes along the sea bed.

Animals of Arctic lands

25 Many kinds of animals live on the lands of the far north. Most of them have thick fur or feathers to keep out the cold and wind in winter. In spring, they shed (moult) their winter fur or feathers, and grow a thinner summer coat.

◀ Ptarmigan change their feathers for camouflage, from white in winter to brownish in summer.

26 Snowy owls make nests on the tundra. They lay their eggs in shallow hollows in the ground. The female looks after her chicks while the male finds food.

▶ Snowy owl chicks feed on small animals such as mice, voles, lemmings and young birds.

27 The ptarmigan gets new feathers for winter. In preparation for the colder months, the ptarmigan grows thick, white feathers. These help it to merge into the natural background, which is known as camouflage. Its winter feathers are also warmer than its brown summer feathers.

WHITE ON WHITE

How do snowy owls 'hide' out in the open? Make a snowy owl by cutting out an owl face shape and feathers from white paper. Draw the eyes and beak. Hold the owl in front of surfaces of different colours. See how it stands out more against dark colours and less against pale colours.

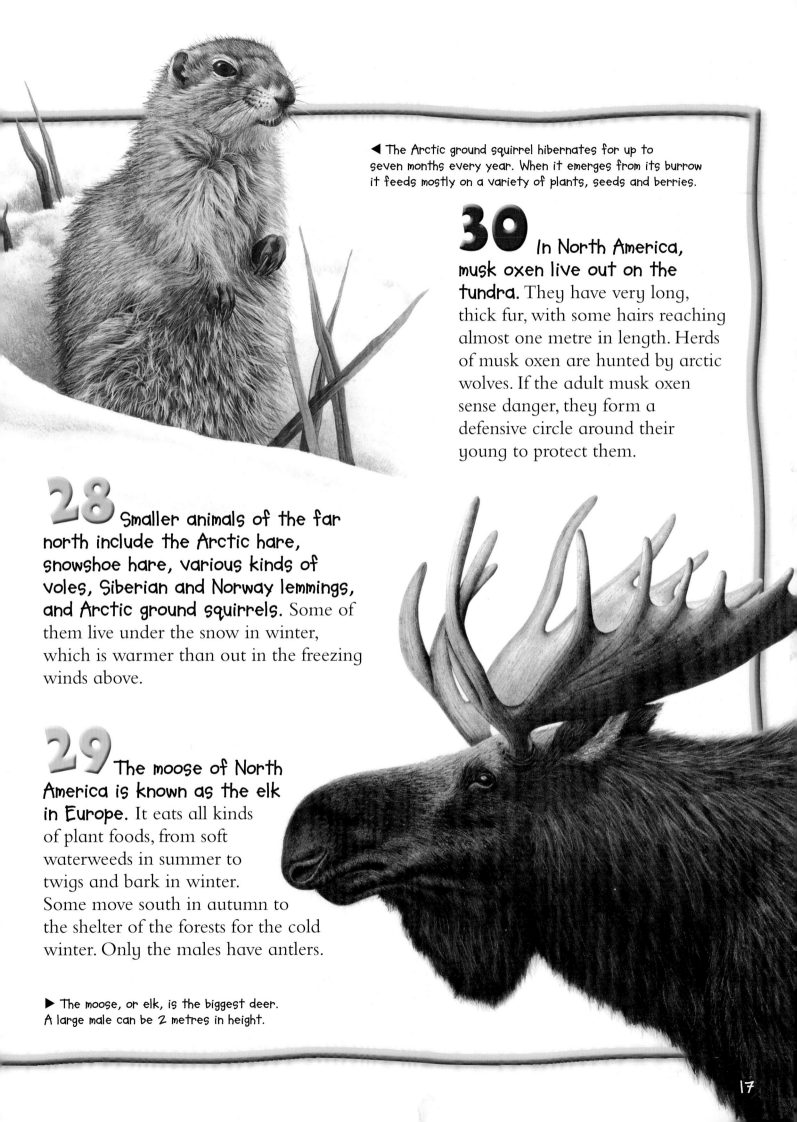

◀ The Arctic ground squirrel hibernates for up to seven months every year. When it emerges from its burrow it feeds mostly on a variety of plants, seeds and berries.

30 In North America, musk oxen live out on the tundra. They have very long, thick fur, with some hairs reaching almost one metre in length. Herds of musk oxen are hunted by arctic wolves. If the adult musk oxen sense danger, they form a defensive circle around their young to protect them.

28 Smaller animals of the far north include the Arctic hare, snowshoe hare, various kinds of voles, Siberian and Norway lemmings, and Arctic ground squirrels. Some of them live under the snow in winter, which is warmer than out in the freezing winds above.

29 The moose of North America is known as the elk in Europe. It eats all kinds of plant foods, from soft waterweeds in summer to twigs and bark in winter. Some move south in autumn to the shelter of the forests for the cold winter. Only the males have antlers.

▶ The moose, or elk, is the biggest deer. A large male can be 2 metres in height.

Realm of bears and wolves

▲ Arctic foxes often follow polar bears, to feed on the leftover bits of their kill.

31 The biggest land hunter in the Arctic, and in the world, is the polar bear. However it often hunts in water and on ice, too! A big male polar bear can measure 3 metres in length and weigh over half a tonne.

32 The polar bear's favourite food is seals. Camouflaged against the snow, polar bears hunt by creeping up on their prey, then pouncing. They also wait by seals' breathing holes for one to appear above the water. Then the bear bites the seal or hooks it out of the water with its huge claws.

I DON'T BELIEVE IT!

Mother polar bears are enormous, weighing as much as four adult humans, but cubs are tiny, weighing around half a kilogram – that's only one-eighth of the weight of a human baby.

34 Wolves of the far north tend to follow their prey, such as caribou and musk oxen, until it tires. Wolves work in packs to kill a large victim, or they can hunt alone for smaller prey such as Arctic hares, voles and lemmings.

▶ In midwinter, the mother polar bear gives birth to two or three tiny babies, called cubs, in a snow cave she digs.

33 Polar bears can swim for hours in icy water, and walk across land, ice or frozen snow. Their fur is very thick, and their paws are wide so they sink less in soft snow. They also have a layer of fat under their skin, called blubber, which keeps in body heat.

▼ Wolves try to break up and scatter a herd of musk oxen so they can attack the young.

35 Only the chief male and female of the wolf pack (the alpha pair), mate and have cubs. Other pack members help look after the cubs, and bring them food. They also help to defend the pack from polar bears and brown bears.

Arctic seals

36 **Many kinds of seals live in the Arctic region.** These include ringed seals, bearded seals, harp seals, spotted seals, ribbon seals and hooded seals. Most feed on fish, squid and small shrimp-like creatures called krill, which are also eaten by whales.

◀ Seals make breathing holes by bashing their noses, teeth and flippers against the thin ice.

37 **Seals have very thick fur to keep out the cold water.** Like their main enemy, the polar bear, they also have a layer of fatty blubber under the skin to keep them warm. They swim well but have to come up to breathe every few minutes. Sometimes they use breathing holes they make in the ice.

38 **In spring, mother seals come onto the ice to give birth.** Their babies, or pups, have very thick, fluffy fur to keep them warm. Each mother seal usually has only one pup. She feeds it on very rich milk, and it grows very quickly.

▼ Walruses often use their flippers and tusks to haul themselves out of the water onto rocky shores, to sunbathe during the brief summer.

39 Mother seals have to return to the water to feed, leaving their pups alone on the ice. At this time pups are in danger from polar bears, wolves and other predators. Within a couple of weeks the young seal is big enough to look after itself.

40 The walrus is a huge seal with two long upper teeth, called tusks. It shows these off at breeding time to impress its partner. Tusks are also used in feeding, to lever shellfish off the seabed. A big walrus can grow to 3 metres in length and weigh 1.5 tonnes!

Whales of the far north

42 The beluga is also called the white whale. It makes a variety of sounds such as whistles, squeals, twitters and chirps. These can be heard even above the surface. Old-time sailors nicknamed it the 'sea canary'. Both the beluga and narwhal are 4 to 6 metres in length and weigh about one tonne. They eat prey such as fish, squid and shellfish.

▲ The beluga whale has very bendy lips, and purses them as though kissing, to suck in its food.

43 The beluga and narwhal migrate within the Arctic, from the southern areas of the Arctic Ocean to the even icier waters further north. They follow the edge of the ice sheet as it shrinks each spring, then grows back again each autumn.

41 The cold seas of the Arctic are visited in summer by many kinds of whales, including the biggest of all, the blue whale. However, there are some whales that stay in the Arctic all year round, such as the beluga and narwhal.

I DON'T BELIEVE IT!

The massive bowhead whale has the largest head and mouth of any animal. Its head is almost one-third of its 18 metre-long-body. The brush-like baleen strips in its huge curved mouth can be more than 4 metres in length!

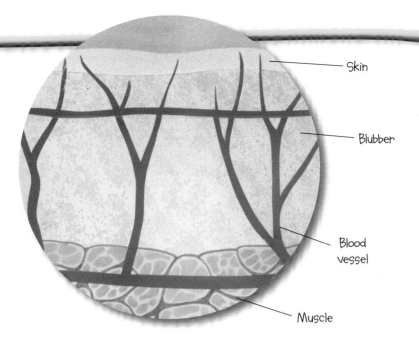

Skin

Blubber

Blood vessel

Muscle

▲ Whales, seals and other polar mammals have a thick layer of blubber under their skin. In whales it is about five times thicker than the fat beneath human skin.

44 The male narwhal has a tooth in its upper jaw that grows very long and pointed, to form a spear-like tusk. This can reach 3 metres in length. It is sometimes used to pierce a hole in the ice so the whale can come up to breathe.

45 The northern right and the bowhead whale are baleen whales. They have long brush-like fringes of baleen in their mouths to filter tiny animals, called plankton, from the sea. These whales can weigh up to 80 tonnes! They are among the world's rarest whales, with just a few hundred right whales left.

46 One of the most powerful Arctic hunters is the killer whale, or orca. It is not a true whale, but the largest kind of dolphin. It lives in large family groups called pods and hunts fish, seals and even great whales.

▶ At breeding time, male narwhals use their tusks to battle with each other.

Summer visitors

47 Some animals migrate north to the Arctic for its short summer. At this time, Arctic days are long and food is plentiful. In autumn, as the long winter approaches, animals return south to warmer regions.

48 The Arctic tern has the longest migration of all animals. It breeds in summer at the Arctic, then follows the warm weather south to the Antarctic, to have another summer. It covers an amazing 35,000 kilometres every year.

▼ The Arctic tern swoops down to the sea's surface to eat small creatures such as baby fish and krill.

▼ Snow geese flock to the tundra of North America in huge family groups, where each pair raises three to five chicks.

49

The mighty sperm whale is also a summer visitor to the Arctic. The huge males swim from the tropics to the edge of the pack ice. They dive to great depths to catch fish and giant squid.

▲ Grey whale babies (calves) join their mothers on the long journey north each spring, but many are attacked by sharks and killer whales.

50

Many kinds of geese and other birds migrate to the Arctic in summer, such as snow geese, Brent geese and barnacle geese. These birds make nests and rear their chicks quickly. They feed on grasses, rushes, sedges and other plants of the boggy tundra, as well as eating flies, grubs and other small creatures from pools along the seashore.

51

Grey whales swim along the coasts of the North Atlantic in spring, to feed in the waters off Alaska and in the Bering Sea throughout the summer. Then they return to subtropical waters off Baja California, Mexico, and spend the winter resting and giving birth. Their yearly journeys total 20,000 kilometres, and are the longest migration of any mammal.

QUIZ

Do some research and see if you can put these animals in order of the distance they cover on their yearly migration:

A Bowhead whale
B Barnacle goose
C Sperm whale
D Arctic tern
E Caribou

Answers:
D C B E A

In the Southern Ocean

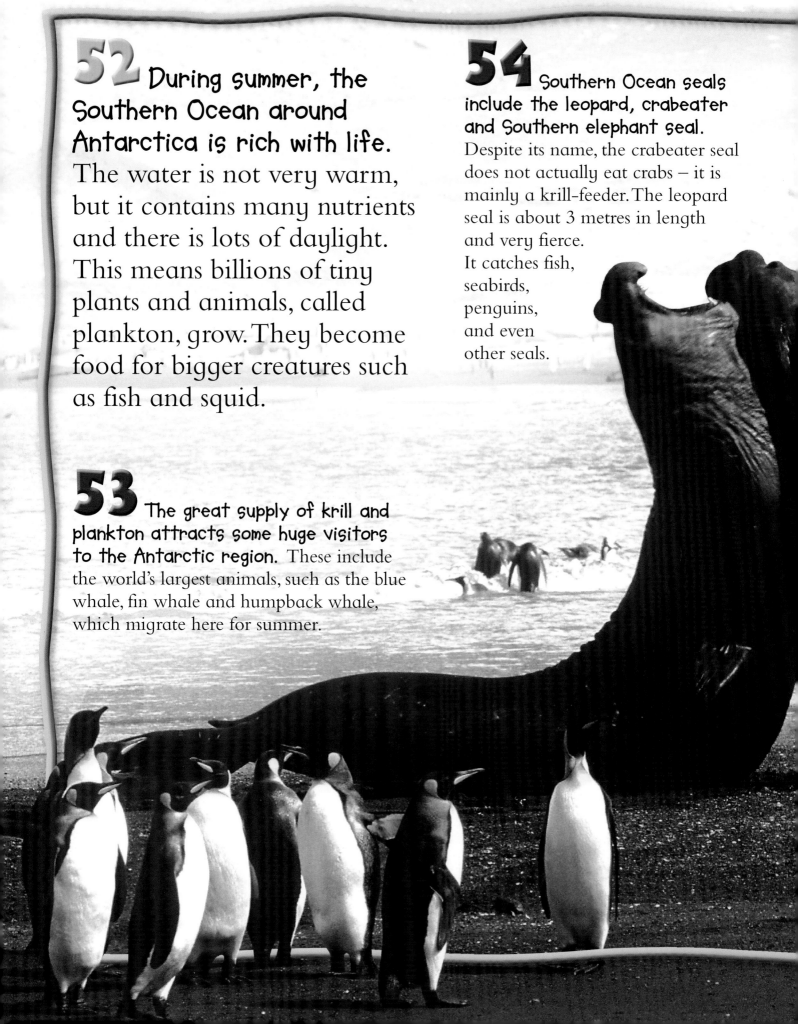

52 During summer, the Southern Ocean around Antarctica is rich with life. The water is not very warm, but it contains many nutrients and there is lots of daylight. This means billions of tiny plants and animals, called plankton, grow. They become food for bigger creatures such as fish and squid.

53 The great supply of krill and plankton attracts some huge visitors to the Antarctic region. These include the world's largest animals, such as the blue whale, fin whale and humpback whale, which migrate here for summer.

54 Southern Ocean seals include the leopard, crabeater and Southern elephant seal. Despite its name, the crabeater seal does not actually eat crabs – it is mainly a krill-feeder. The leopard seal is about 3 metres in length and very fierce. It catches fish, seabirds, penguins, and even other seals.

55 A Southern elephant seal is almost as big as a real elephant! These seals spend weeks at sea feeding, then come to remote beaches to breed. The huge males, called beachmasters, rear up, roaring and biting each other, before mating with the females.

▼ Male elephant seals battle each other to win an area of the beach, otherwise they do not breed. Sometimes they become badly injured in the fight, and die.

56 Elephant seals are the deepest-diving of all seals. They can dive down more than 1000 metres and stay under the water for over an hour before they need to surface for breath. They eat mainly fish and squid, as well as crabs and shrimps from the ocean floor.

I DON'T BELIEVE IT!

A male southern elephant seal can be more than 5 metres in length. When it is well fed, it weighs almost two tonnes! It gets its name from its huge size, and from its long, floppy nose.

Antarctic waters

57 Apart from seals, whales, fish and squid, many other creatures thrive in Antarctic waters. They include jellyfish that drift with the currents, trailing their long tentacles. The tentacles sting passing creatures, which are then pulled up to the mouth on the underside of the jellyfish's umbrella-like body (bell).

58 The temperature of polar seas often falls below 0°C. However, the waters do not always freeze, so animals are safe from being frozen solid. This is because sea water contains salts, so its freezing point is lower than fresh water. Ice crystals also break up as they form, due to the movement of the seas' currents and waves.

▼ The *Isotealia* anemone lives in waters from about 50 to 500 metres deep. It grabs any kind of food, including jellyfish and sea urchins.

▶ The huge desmonema jellyfish grows to more than one metre across. It catches fish, krill, sea worms and starfish.

59 Cousins of jellyfish, known as sea anemones, also live along the coasts of Antarctic islands. They too have stinging tentacles that pull in prey such as shrimps and prawns. However the mainland shores of Antarctica itself are too cold for most kinds of seaside animals.

QUIZ

Do some research to find out which fish is most closely related to the Antarctic ice-fish.

A Flatfish
B Sharks
C Trout
D Perch

Answer: D

60 **Several polar fish have special substances in their blood and body fluids that work like natural anti-freeze.** Even if trapped in solid ice, these animals can survive for a while by going into suspended animation – staying still and using almost no energy.

▶ There are several kinds of Antarctic ice-fish, which have blood that is thickened by certain natural chemicals to stop it freezing.

Antarctic birds

61 Antarctica is visited by hundreds of kinds of birds each year. Most of them fly over the open ocean, since there is very little unfrozen land on which to nest. In contrast, the islands close to Antarctica are home to some breeding birds, such as albatrosses and petrels.

▼ Research scientists measure the wingspan of an albatross.

62 The wandering albatross has longer wings than any other bird, at more than 3 metres from tip to tip. Albatrosses form long-lasting breeding pairs that come together on remote islands to raise their single chick. The young albatross may not fly until it is almost one year old.

▶ Tussock birds are always on the lookout for any morsels of food. This bird is pecking bits of flaking skin from an elephant seal.

63 **The blackish cinclodes, also called the tussock bird, eats almost anything it can find.** It snaps up shellfish and shrimps along the coast and eats dead crabs and starfish washed up on the shore. Tussock birds also wander around seabird colonies to feed on the rotting fish that the parent birds cough up, or regurgitate, for their chicks.

64 **Skuas are powerful seabirds with large, sharp beaks.** They chase terns, gulls and similar birds and attack them in mid air, forcing them to drop their food, which the skua then gulps down.

▶ The skua's strong beak can easily stab into a penguin's egg. Then the bird laps up the soft inner parts or hacks apart the chick inside.

Sliding and diving

65 **Penguins live only in the south, around Antarctica – there are none in the Arctic.** They cannot fly, but they use their flipper-like wings to swim with great speed and skill. Most of the 17 kinds of penguins live on the islands and shores of the Southern Ocean, on the icebergs and ice floes there, and on the continent of Antarctica itself.

▼ Penguins' outer feathers overlap in water or when the weather is cold, and stand upright when it is warmer.

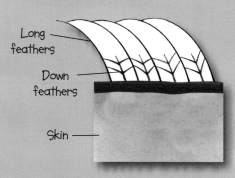

1. Long feathers overlap, trapping warm air next to the skin

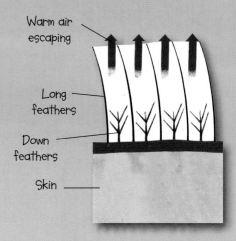

2. Long feathers separate, letting warm air escape

66 **The biggest penguins are emperors.** They can be up to 120 centimetres in height and weigh more than 30 kilograms. They breed on Antarctic ice, and the female lays just one egg, passes it over to the male, and leaves. She sets off on the long journey back to the sea to feed.

▶ Adelie penguins slide down an icy cliff and take to the water, in search of their main food – krill.

67 The male emperor penguin spends almost two months of the worst midwinter weather with the egg on his feet, keeping it warm until it hatches. Then the female returns, walking and sliding across the ice, to take over caring for the chick. At last the hungry male can head to the sea to feed.

68 The king penguin is the second-largest penguin. It stands about 90 centimetres in height and weighs up to 15 kilograms. Its main foods are fish, squid and plankton. King penguins can dive down to 200 metres.

▲ Emperor penguins travel to traditional breeding sites to find a partner and mate. When an egg hatches, the parent bird brings up (regurgitates) food from its stomach to feed its chick.

33

Polar peoples

69 People have lived in Arctic regions for over 10,000 years. Today, groups exist around northern North America, Scandinavia (northern Europe) and Siberia (north Asia). They include Inuit, Aleuts, Koryak, and Chukchi people. They live in some of the world's most difficult conditions.

70 In recent times, the traditional way of life in polar regions has changed greatly. New ways of travel are available, from skidoos and other snowmobiles to helicopters, snowplanes and icebreaker ships. Many polar people are no longer cut off from the lands farther south. They can trade more easily for consumer goods such as clothes, tools, TVs and prepared foods.

▼ Snowmobiles have skis at the front for steering, and tracks at the rear to push the vehicle along. Here, a Saami person crosses a snow-covered lake in Finland.

71 Commercial fishing is big business in some Arctic areas. Ships catch large numbers of fish or krill, especially in summer. Whaling and sealing are banned, but ships continue to catch food that these animals eat, so the populations can still be harmed.

ski-doo

▶ Traditional fishing skills are still vital. This man is fishing for halibut through a hole in the ice in Greenland.

72 **One of the most helpful modern items for northern people has been the gun.** In the past, spears or hooks and lines were used to catch seals and other food. Even when using guns, hunters still need patience. Arctic animals are very wary and it is difficult to creep up on them unseen in the white, icy wilderness.

▼ Tourism is a growing business in Ilulissat, Greenland, a World Heritage Site. Visitors come to see icebergs breaking off the Sermeq Kujalleq glacier.

73 **The discovery of oil, coal, minerals and other resources have brought many newcomers to the Arctic.** Settlements have grown up along the coasts. The houses are heated by oil, from wells in the area, or coal mined locally, since there are no trees to burn as fuel.

Living in the cold

74 Over time, Arctic people have developed skills and knowledge to survive in this harsh environment. Plants are scarce, so food is mainly animals such as seals, shellfish, fish and whales. A stranded whale can provide enough food for a week.

75 Arctic animals provide not just food, but many other resources for polar people. The fatty blubber is burned in lamps for heat and warmth. Weatherproof clothes and boots are made from the furry skins of seals, caribou and other creatures.

76 Tools and utensils such as knives, bowls and spoons are also made from local animals. They are carved from the bones and teeth of smaller toothed whales, from the horns of caribou and musk oxen, from the tusks of walrus and narwhals, and from the bendy, springy baleen or whalebone of great whales.

1. Large blocks of squashed snow or loose ice are cut with a large-bladed snow-knife.

2. The blocks are stacked in a circular pattern, sloping inwards in a gradually rising spiral.

3. The blocks slope together to make a dome shape that keeps out wind and snow.

◀ Snow houses called igloos are usually a temporary shelter, made for just a night or two while out on a winter hunting expedition.

▶ Kayaks are usually paddled by hand with paddles made from driftwood. Some modern ones have outboard motors. Here, a kayak is launched by hunters in Alaska.

77

Since so much food is obtained from the sea, boats are very useful. The canoe-like kayak is made by stretching waterproof animal skin such as whale hide over a frame of carved driftwood, or perhaps bone. The parts are tied together with animal sinews.

78

Kayaks are light and easily carried, and slide well across snow and ice. Larger kayaks are used for carrying a family's possessions to a new hunting area.

◀ The joints between the blocks in an igloo are sealed with snow to keep out the wind. The entrance is low down to prevent the warm air inside from escaping.

QUIZ

Try and find out which materials Antarctic people use to make the following items:

A. Boots
B. An overcoat
C. A head-dress

Answers:
A. Waterproof sealskin
B. Reindeer hide
C. Seabird feathers

Life of a herder

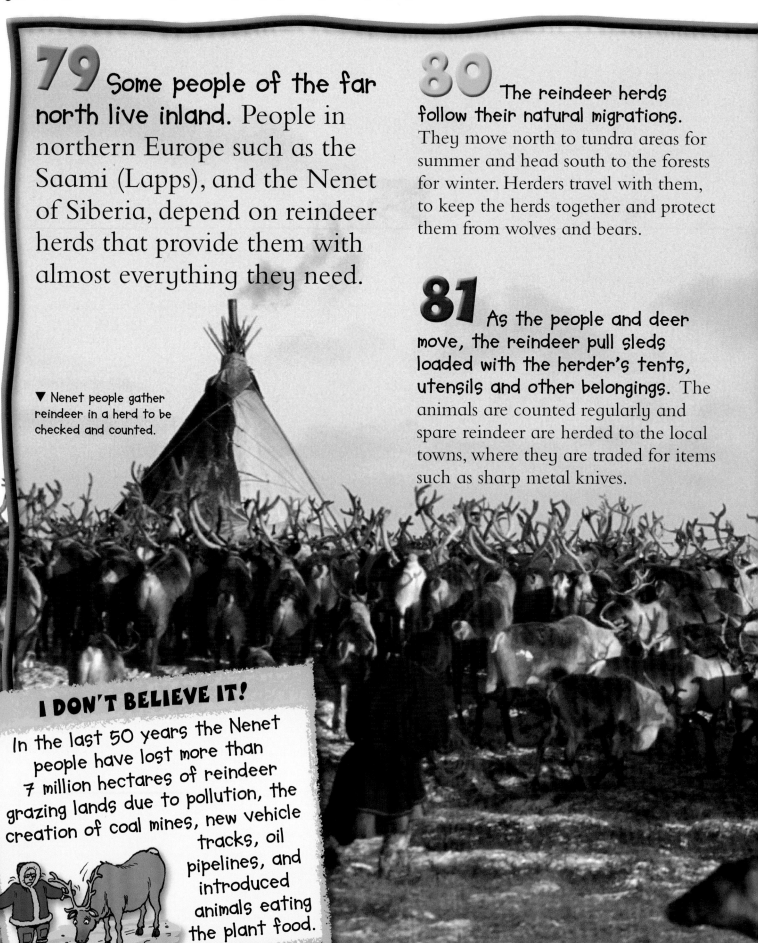

79 **Some people of the far north live inland.** People in northern Europe such as the Saami (Lapps), and the Nenet of Siberia, depend on reindeer herds that provide them with almost everything they need.

▼ Nenet people gather reindeer in a herd to be checked and counted.

80 **The reindeer herds follow their natural migrations.** They move north to tundra areas for summer and head south to the forests for winter. Herders travel with them, to keep the herds together and protect them from wolves and bears.

81 **As the people and deer move, the reindeer pull sleds loaded with the herder's tents, utensils and other belongings.** The animals are counted regularly and spare reindeer are herded to the local towns, where they are traded for items such as sharp metal knives.

I DON'T BELIEVE IT!

In the last 50 years the Nenet people have lost more than 7 million hectares of reindeer grazing lands due to pollution, the creation of coal mines, new vehicle tracks, oil pipelines, and introduced animals eating the plant food.

82 Reindeer can provide a huge variety of resources. Their fur and skins make clothes, boots, floor rugs, sleeping blankets and tents. They provide fresh milk and blood to drink, and their meat is very nutritious. The antlers and bones are carved into utensils and tools. They are also used, along with teeth, to make beautiful works of art, showing scenes of fishing, hunting, herding and the natural world.

▲ Saami hunters live in tents of reindeer hide stretched over log poles, which can be easily packed and transported by sled.

On top of the world!

83 Many adventurers have tried to reach the North Pole, which is located near the middle of a floating layer of ice in the Arctic Ocean. Before today's satellite navigation, it was hard to know if you were in the right place. Then, explorers had to prove that they really did reach their destination. They couldn't leave a flag in the floating, breaking ice.

▶ Nansen's ship *Fram* was stuck in ice for almost three years, but its design meant that it survived.

84 English admiral William Parry tried to reach the North Pole in 1825. So did Norwegian explorer Fridtjof Nansen in 1893–96 in his ship *Fram*. Yet neither of them made it. In 1909, American Robert Peary and his team claimed to have reached the North Pole, but experts do not agree if they really did.

85 The first people to fly over the North Pole in a plane may have been Richard Byrd and Floyd Bennet in 1926. However, as with Peary, it's not certain if they really did. A few days later, Roald Amundsen – the first person to reach the South Pole – flew over the North Pole in an airship, the *Norge*.

◀ Some experts disagree with Robert Peary's claim that he marched across the floating ice to the North Pole.

86 Claims to be first to stand at the North Pole continued, such as Russian explorer Pavel Gordiyenko and his team in 1952. In 1968, American explorer Ralph Plaisted and two colleagues made the first surface trip there.

87 In modern times, more and more expeditions have reached the North Pole across the ice. In 2007, Dutch performer Guido van der Werve spent a day there, turning in the opposite direction to the Earth's spinning, so in fact he stayed completely still. It is even possible for rich tourists to fly to the exact North Pole for a few hours' visit.

▼ In 2007, Lewis Gordon Pugh swam one kilometre through water in cracks between the North Pole ice, to highlight the problem of global warming.

Race to the South Pole

89 Once ships arrived at Antarctica, there was still a dangerous journey across the ice to the South Pole. Irish explorer Ernest Shackleton made several trips there. In 1901–02 in the ship *Discovery*, and in 1914–16 in *Endurance*. These trips did not reach the South Pole, but helped to establish bases for further exploring across the ice cap.

▶ In Ernest Shackelton's 1914–15 expedition, his ship *Endurance* was frozen into the ice for ten months and finally crushed. Yet all the crew were eventually rescued.

88 It was difficult to even get close to the South Pole. In 1820, Russian naval officer Fabian Gottlieb von Bellingshausen was perhaps the first person to see the Antarctic mainland. American seal-hunter John Davis may have been first to set foot on the continent, in 1821. In 1839, English naval commander James Clark Ross set sail on a voyage to map Antarctica's outline. Many of these people have areas of Antarctica named after them.

SLIPPERY SLOPE

You will need:
length of wood   ice cubes
stones   wood   plastic

Hold up one end of the wood, like a ramp. Put an ice cube at the top and let it slide down. The ice melts into water, which works like slippery oil. Try sliding the other substances such as plastic, wood and stone. The ramp has to be much steeper!

▲ Amundsen's expedition saved the weight of carrying food by killing and eating the sled dogs one by one.

90 In 1911 two expeditions set off to reach the South Pole, led by Norwegian Roald Amundsen, and English naval officer Robert Scott. The world was gripped by news of their 'race to the Pole'. Amundsen, his team and his dog sleds got there first on 14 December 1911, and returned safely. Scott and his team, pulling their own sledges, arrived a month later. Tragically, on the way back they ran out of supplies and were stranded by blizzards. They did not survive.

91 The South Pole can now be visited by rich tourists. Several overland expeditions make the trek each year. There is a permanent scientific base called the Amundsen–Scott South Pole Station, where people live and work, usually for a period of six months.

▶ In 1997, mother-of-two Laurence de la Ferriere walked across Antarctica to the South Pole unaided.

Polar lands in peril

92 From about 300 years ago, the polar regions were exploited by anyone who could get there. Vast numbers of seals, whales, fish and squid, as well as other animals were killed. By the 1950s these creatures had become very rare, and in 1980 mass whaling was banned.

93 Valuable resources such as oil, coal and precious minerals were found in polar areas such as Alaska and Siberia. A rush began to dig and drill there. Now, pipelines and oil tankers carry oil and gas thousands of kilometres to major cities.

◀ As polar waters warm slightly, they melt, wearing away the ice shelves, floes and icebergs at a faster rate.

I DON'T BELIEVE IT!

There are many predictions about how fast polar ice will melt and raise sea levels. Some say they will rise by one metre by the year 2100. Even a small rise will flood great cities and make millions homeless.

94 Pollution has begun to affect the polar lands. Dangerous chemicals such as pesticides from farming, and toxins from industry, flow into Arctic waters. The protective ozone layer above Antarctica has been made thinner by chemicals from aerosol spray cans. Oil spills from tankers have devastated parts of the Arctic.

95 Climate change will have terrifying results around the world. The habitats of polar bears, seals, penguins and many other animals are disappearing. Floods will affect low-lying areas far from polar lands, where billions of people live in cities. Polar scientific bases have been set up to study these problems.

▶ Cleaning penguins' coats of pollution strips their feathers of natural oils, without which the birds could freeze to death. Rescued birds are fitted with woolly jumpers to keep them warm.

96 The greatest threat to polar regions may still be to come. Global warming due to the greenhouse effect is causing climate change, as world temperatures rise. This is making the ice caps melt, causing sea levels to rise.

▼ The striped pole marks the exact spot of the South Pole. It is repositioned every New Year's Day, as the ice moves around 10 metres yearly.

Protecting the Poles

97 Countries have signed agreements to protect polar lands and oceans from damage. Even tourism can be a problem. Cruise ships bring visitors that disturb whales and other wildlife, and leave waste.

▼ Scientists monitor emperor penguin breeding colonies near the Weddell Sea, Antarctica, to see the effect of climate change on their breeding.

98 In 1994 the Southern Ocean was declared a vast sanctuary, or safe area, for whales. This meant it was also safe for many other kinds of wildlife. However some countries still hunt whales, and ships also go there to catch krill, fish and squid. As we catch more, whales and other large animals have less to eat.

99 Some parts of the Arctic are also being protected. Some countries want to drill for oil and gas, and mine for coal, precious minerals and metals. Big companies sometimes try to change the minds of governments or break the rules. These activities create jobs for people, but create risks of pollution.

100 The polar lands and oceans are far away from most of us. Yet they are the last great wildernesses on Earth. They have the harshest habitats in the world, where animals have had to adapt or perish. These places need our help to survive.

Index

Entries in **bold** refer to main subject entries. Entries in *italics* refer to illustrations.